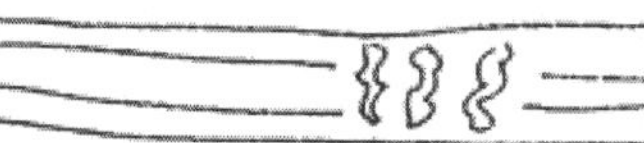

A Modern Classic

HANDWRITTEN BY

Finola Moorhead

ONE AND ONLY COPY

bound book bought by

D.M.F. WILSON
(November 27, 1977)

Herewith ◊◊◊

"The private as the social meeting place."
W. Billeter 26·11·77

NO LIBRARY NO. F.M.

Spinifex Press Pty Ltd
504 Queensberry St
North Melbourne, Victoria 3051
Australia
women@spinifexpress.com.au
www.spinifexpress.com.au

First published by Post Neo, 1982
This edition published by Spinifex Press, 2013

Cover design: Deb Snibson
Cover Photo: B. O'Regan, 1976
Printed by McPherson's Printing Group

National Library of Australia
Cataloguing-in-Publication

Handwritten Modern Classic
Moorhead, Finola.
A handwritten modern classic [electronic resource] / Finola Moorhead.
2nd ed.

Australian prose literature--20th century.
A828.308

Moorhead in '76 Photo by B.O'Regan

Dedication:

To those who understand
To those who know me already
&
ask can they read it
To those with a sense of humour
who also know the tragedy
of it all
To those who didn't expect it
To those who don't expect anything

[illegible]

Introduction:

I haven't begun yet
There's no one else involved
Names where possible will be exact.
Places might be ignored or described
in great detail.
Exaggeration is my fault not my fiction.
Any claim to being a real modern classic
will be denied, disputed & debunked.

The First

The first observation is that the Imagination is how you do what you know. A person who says he is a writer and uses many words to say that imagination beats experience has no imagination, especially if he cannot toss a salad, lets his wife buy his clothes. Looking at him you know he's tight-arsed and what he's hooked on is the phantasy extension of his own ego. Secretly he wants to write pornography, but he can't, because he's shit-scared — & — beware, dear reader, of giving him your sympathy. It makes you as bad as he is, I'm sorry. Everybody writes pornography in their heads. Enough of Art lost in the damp must of the cramped, anachronistic modern mind!

Neurosis is a handwritten modern classic.
Neurosis is a blockage in the lung.
Neurosis is cancer of the larynx.

Neurosis is an obsession with jogging 12 miles a day in a brand new adidas track suit, buying a bicycle machine and installing air conditioning.

Being a victim is watching too much television.
Being a victim is bickering at the breakfast table.
Being a victim is thinking of taking therapy.
Being a victim is touching your sexual organs in a public place imagining your clothes are hiding this activity.
Being a victim is not knowing what to do with yr. leisure.
Being a victim is doing much the same thing every weekend.
Being a victim is doing the same thing every weekend because you bought a speedboat.
Being a victim is saying things like "It's too late..."
Being a victim is thinking there's something to lose.

Toasting failure is celebrating freedom.
Toasting failure is not a sad thing.
Most toasts are a sad thing.

Toast-makers are goons at whom most people are not permitted to laugh at aloud.

Toast-makers therefore have to make wet jokes and pause after them, otherwise a number of individuals in the audience would burst.

Bursting in the wrong place and spilling your drink and wetting your pants is not the done thing, because it's an embarrassing thing.

An embarrassing thing is when you amuse others & they are not permitted to show it.

Those who are good at not showing it are pillars of society.

Pillars of society are people without a sense of humour.

Pillars of society lack most of the valuable qualities.

Pillars of society are not to be felt sorry for.

Pillars of society crumble when they wet their pants in public unless it's at a dirty party, it's a leak if the public gets to know about it and a leak grows into a scandal, and they worry about that. Perhaps this accounts for the instance of hypertension

Sufferers of hypertension are not to be felt sorry for.
Worried people who are toasting failure are not toasting failure.

Being a victim is not necessarily being a loser.
Being a loser is not necessarily being a victim.
Losers learn faster.

The Romantic listens only to the dead. You must be dead before a romantic will hear you. A romantic thinks he knows Beethoven, Keats, Tolstoy and Blake personally. Romantics rarely read Coleridge's Theory Of The Imagination or Tolstoy's Ressurection. I don't know why. I don't think they were on the syllabus. Romantics are not only literary people. all people who are victims of Sentiment are romantic.
Sentiment is sugar on the shit. Sentiment makes people sick in the marrow of their bones. Romantics don't feel in the marrow of their bones.
"Feeling in the marrow of my bones" is romance / a romantic statement.

It is customary for a Romantic not to know what he's talking about. If a romantic is talking about Truth it is likely to be false. Romantics are very sure. A romantic is a talker not a conversationalist. A romantic cannot exchange ideas because he only listens to the dead. A romantic is a victim of manipulation protesting loudly that he is free. He believes in sin because he needs a word to describe what he does most of the time. The romantic does not understand what the dead are saying to him.

romantic in a country graveyard listening to the dead: "mr. r. you are a great writer, too. Wait 'till you're dead. all you need to do is to insure your private papers."

Romantics are also stubborn.

Examples of how to start:

a) She realised Jack wasn't going to keep his promise. For a moment her eyes lost focus, her hands lay forgotten in the cooling dish water in the sink...

b) They had been here before. Eerily the old store with the verandah posts looked familiar, even the wind blowing autumn leaves down the street was familiar. She recalled an uneasiness in her veins ...

c) If he could only find the joint. He took a gulp from last night's flagon. Coffee would have to be black, instant, hot. He had not heard. No time. Hit the streets...

d) I waited. I grew weak from waiting. An old man sat beside me on the park bench & began talking. And this is the tale he told ...

e) Everyone else believed in ghosts, but I was the

skeptic. Didn't keep my opinions to myself either. This strange assignment had me baffled, the editor knew it. The old man had a slice of mischief about him, perhaps that's why we were a happy mob up at the Paper...

ENOUGH,

dear friends,

you don't want to know what happens next.

dear friends,

sometimes i visit your chaos and i'm troubled by order. Sometimes i have to scream DON'T BE SO SLACK. Yet i've seen you judge me, too. I take and measure out my gift. I sit down with you & i try to think. I walk up to a policeman & i try to think. Nothing seems so important as the anxiety rising right inside me. Suddenly i've got most intimate worries on my mind, when they at any moment they might come & drag me off the road & arrest me for obstructing traffic. I am among strangers protesting about the freeway: FREE, NO WAY. What is the meaning of sacrifice, of difficulty, of work? (No wonder we speak our thoughts so rarely!) Are you sure you're not walled up in a box? Don't think i blame you, i am your friend after all and when questions of loyalty and solidarity come up, i promise you i'll think about it.

Spoken to a room full of romantics:
"You can learn how not to make mistakes, but you can't learn to think. Perhaps you can learn the habits of thinking (then you must unlearn all habits lest they define you.) Writers often only think about writing, writing writing and how what is written is written. And that's not thinking & telling isn't thinking & learning isn't thinking. Reading can mean thinking. So can watching &

listening. Mean it in terms of not only remembering but PLUS Analysis alone is not what thinking is about. You ask why and analysis is a help. But thinking has got to include the instinct, the intuition and the inspiration. Because thinking is revolutionary if it's related to care and if care is related to justice & not to the facile fulfilments of self. Because most of those if you don't think are dictated by society."

Dear Mr Romantic,

a handwritten modern classic is not just writing to hear yourself talk. You misunderstood my meaning of selfish. Understandably, ego-gratification is the air you breathe. Your own selfishness surrounds you so completely you see everything in its light, including the meaning of selfish. What you see is something like selfish squared but mostly obscured so you think it's a little triangle i.e you in front of your shaving mirror reciting a poem you remember every word of which was written in your student days to a person to whom you never really spoke. No, a handwritten modern classic is a pain. Specificaly a pain in my right thumb. What's a missing digit to a real artist?

What's interesting with words is the way they're used gives a person away every time.

What is written is not always what is read.
What is written might never be read.
What is read might never be understood.
What is understood might never be written.
What is understood is never forgotten.
What is remembered in words might easily
be forgotten.

What is understood is never just words.

Words recited for no purpose mean nothing.
Words mean what they say only in the context
of their circumstance.
The circumstance of the recitation which not
a performance is the circumstance of hearing
your voice — not the words — not unless
you haven't understood what they, the
words, are communicating yet, and you
are trying to, and instead of having to
read them over & over again, you have
committed them to memory by rote so
that you can consider their possible meaning
at your leisure.
I do not include nonsense.
Nonsense has a function of its own.
You should not be ashamed of nonsense
as nonsense
You should be ashamed if you think your
nonsense is sense.

Words are prone to the abuse of nonsense.
Understanding is not.

Nonsense is a challenge to the understanding.
If the understanding fails that doesn't matter.
If the understanding succeeds then sense is made and the nonsence is rearticulated in a different form.
Nonsense need not challenge the understanding.
Nonsence may be understanding in another circumstance.
Nonsense should not be confused with sence.
Sense & understanding are not necessarily the same thing.
Sense may be articulated.
Understanding need not.
Noncense may be articulated.
Articulation is not necessarily sense.
Articulation has to do with words.
Sense has to do with words in logical relationship with each other.

The logical relationships of words with each other is not necessarily strictly grammatical.
Grammar is a chosen form not God the Father of verbal language.
Grammar has had to be fairly logical or otherwise it wouldn't have survived.
That which has to be learnt by rote is forgotten soon afterwards.

Survival of language requires understanding.
Understanding is born of the experience of meaning.
Understanding is an experience.
To sacrifice the experience of understanding for some predetermined ego-gratification is what is generally expected of the individual in this society.
Romantic fiction or romanticised stories of reality are a form of predetermined ego-gratification.
True stories which do not go beyond the reality of being a victim in this society are just as bad.

Romantic fiction needs only to be thought about to the point of dismissal.

Note: the existential simple sentence is an aid to logic. Logic using simple elements is capable of complexity. Logic isn't all.

Simplicity is a dream in the present environment.

The Second

The irrelevancy ~~tt~~ of this document is matched by its freedom & difficulty. The irrelevancy is determined as much by its physical form as its literary formality. I feel very formal writing a handwritten modern classic.

This morning is Monday the twenty-eighth of November in the year of Jesu Christo Nineteen hundred & seventy-seven. 'Seventy seven jaks make a horse woman,' my sister said to me when i was seven.

There's a battle raging down the street. The State Government's Board of Country Roads has built an expensive freeway. The inner suburbs are trying to stop it opening by building barricades of old car bodies, 'fridges, beds and theatre seats. The CRB is now protected by an enormous detail of policemen. There's a political confrontation at the bottom of my

Hey Mr Romantic, intimate of Lord Byron, the revolution's right here in Collingwood & made up of the banal needs of daily life. The spontaneous expression of the people who haven't a say in the air they breathe.

I have a grievance. Policemen who offer my dog sweet biscuits from their tea-wagon are not to be felt sorry for. Don't feed someone else's dog. Don't feed dogs sweet things.

Judith you are not even a good copy of Mr Romantic. If I could only give an idea of the picture of your ~~expression~~ expression when I said in the seminar, 'not for you to lead western thought.' 'Do you,' she asked, 'mean yourself or all of us?' Well, writers. 'That doesn't include me and I'd like to say on behalf of the others here that we do lead western thought.' Chris Mann yelled from the

back, 'on behalf of me you don't.'
Your presence did not look me in the eye. Your shoulders held high, your legs crossed, your body at a prim twist, stiffened with disapproval. You had not heard me at all. I let my nervousness be swamped by passion. "Maybe," i continued my talk, 'you make a contribution if it's squeezed out between the encroaching blocks of your despair (powered by your thought) and your buoyant creativity (powered by passion) and pushed from behind by the fact that you haven't committed suicide yet, and you choose to survive in this humiliating consumerist world, hopefully with some dignity & health.'

You, i know, keep the handwritten versions of your dreadful poems because you believe one day the National Library in Canberra will be interested - but the handwritten version has a very short life as the only copy. Once it's achieved boom you go to you typewriter back the pages with carbon just in case & with the delicious certainty of repetition you type it out. A copy for the magazine, a copy for your folder, the ms of your next slim volume and one somewhere for safe keeping. The little old ladies in the audience who never get published were not shocked or insulted by my talk, they thought i was on their side. Not you Judith.

You are not to be felt sorry for, dear.

My meaning of Romantic is not to be confused with Romanticism, the academic term which describes a few poets & composers of a certain time.

The Artist as Hero is not a chapter.
The Artist as Coward is not a chapter either.
The Artist as anything different from the rest is to

deny the artist common humanity.
The question of genius is an irrelevant one.

Mad Dave, a Carlton eccentric, has just passed me in the street commenting that my talk on Saturday was very religious.
Fine.
This interpretation is one of the joys of the art.
Back to genius. Because it is so irrelevant, people enjoy talking nonsense about it. Anything that is irrelevant can entertain a group of thoroughly boring people for hours. The fact of entertainment is not irrelevant. Life itself.
The tawdry entertainment gone in for in this society is an interesting sociological fact & should not be ignored.
It should be considered to the point of dismissal.
I am now writing the handwritten modern classic in Lygon St. and although my feet are suffering pins & needles, i find it a congenial atmosphere.

⚘

The Third

Peter K. has a whining voice. He's more of an old duck than you, dea ladies in the lounge.

Dear ladies-in-the-lounge, you are older & you imagine that it would be better having an intelligent man to talk to. Why do you blame each other? Your blame keeps you separate from one another and magnifies the ravages made by men on each of you — one even has a bandaid over the left eye. Your bitter words come from a diet of falsity. Now i've finished this glass of beer. Goodnight.

The Fourth

Perfection has to do with classical. (That is not to say a modern classic is classical or perfect.) In fact any adjective plus classic is imperfect. Perfection, believe it or not, is a Romantic term precisely because it is unattainable and unreal. It has to be romantic. I no longer have faith in the ultimate or the wholeness of things. Whole is here and now and chaotic and fragmentary. Whole is not necessarily perfect. To finish does not mean to perfect. Actually a finished thing if it is real cannot be perfect. Who cares? Perfection, nah.

On the other hand, no blame. We deal in realities and perceptions, with vision & blindness. We deal with magnanimity and forgiveness. There is no righteous punishment. Punishment cannot perfect. Punishment is political. Matters of right and wrong are matters of your politics — accordingly, something to die for.

Martyrdom is a matter of politics.
There is no perfection in death.
Mourn those who died for a bit of pie in the
sky. Joe Hill. ♫ 'I never died said he'

Classical perfection is a matter of symmetry.
Something of similar symmetry may not achieve
perfection. Classical is a matter of time gone by.
For perfection substitute endurance.

CORRECT

Correct has to do with rules.
Rules have to do with how a thing is done obediently.
Rules are some one else's politics.
It is correct to have imagination & do away with rules.
Conflict is excellent.
It is political to find out where exactly the conflict lies.
It is useful not to put your imagination out to
graze on the green grass of phantasy.
Dreams & phantasy have no connection.
Imaginative politics may seem like daydreams.
Daydreams require dedication, work & courage to

become effective politics.
It is political to handwrite a modern classic, though it doesn't seem to be.
Phantasy is no escape.
Phantasy is escape from escape. i.e. avoiding the responsibility of escape.

Escape is a responsibility if you are gaoled in another's reality.
The responsibility of escape is a political reality.
Most victims are unaware of their insanity.
Common insanity is mistaken for normality.
In such a case the quality of human nature falls below par.
At least those who are clinically mad can see the walls of the institution.
Seeing solid walls with as many senses as possible is being hospitalised or gaoled.
This is not desirable.
It is political to escape.
One's policy should resemble sanity.

Physical freedom resembles freedom.
Few are even physically free.
There are too many rules & duties.
There is not enough imagination.
There is insufficient imagination because most
people are mad.
Madness impairs faculties &
imagination is forced to work on what
is not, not what is.
Imagination is best employed on what is.
To escape one's own experience is to immediately
pervert & distort the imagination.
The imagination is the first to feel trapped,
then perhaps you forget things.
To exist in a world of your own is have no
world of your own.
Late at night is the time to write these things.
To feel alienated is a common complaint.
Common alienation is a common hindrance
to communication.
There is not much communication these days.

beyond rules, duties and propaganda.
The transmitting of one's private world onto the airwaves, into an art or within conversation is a romantic view of communication.
When all's said & done it's an arm of propaganda.
Communication should be an aide to freedom.
Communication, understanding & knowledge are in freedom.
All steps in freedom have to do with thought.
Thought alone is not freedom.
Action has to do with choices, choices are aided by thought.
Thought, feeling & intuition shouldn't be understood as different entities.
If one is a victim of one's feelings then one's feelings are not free.
Unfree feelings are divorced from their source.
Emotions are not unrelated to everything.
In the common insanity emotions are bottlenecked.
Such intensity is false & an aid to madness.

Frustration is a Rightist plot.
Frustration is as much an aspect of "normality" as its suppression.
Normality is a neurotic mess.
It is political to change normality.

The Fifth

One is not to not consider Jane Austen sarcastic. A fair reading of Jane Austen is only had after one has confronted sarcasm.

Romantics hate sarcasm. Romantics consider themselves superior to cynics. Romantics are only superior to cynics in that they can protect themselves from devastation by truth. Cynics are rarer. Even so cynicism & sarcasm are not to be confused.
Sarcasm is a method of criticism with a sharp edge.
Cynicism is the acreage on which despair & hope have wrought their civil war.
Cynicism that comprehends neither hope nor despair is a kind of inverted romanticism.
Usually Romantics thinks themselves benevolent.
A cynical Romantic is malevolent.
Good & evil are both a matter of romantic distortion.
A sarcasm such as Jane Austen's has considerable

moral intention.
If one bothers to be sarcastic, one bothers.

Sarcasm displayed for increased power by the forces of Right is downright cruel & destructive.
Sarcasm if employed as an aide must be thought about carefully, the essence being humanity.
If one is inhumane one has no right to be sarcastic, and likely as not, utterly humourless.
To be effectively sarcastic one must be compassionate.

I am too scared to live in this police state. The installation down at Brunswick St. now includes an enormous cyclone fence, three to five lines of vehicles including buses, paddywagons, horse-floats, dog-vans and many white squad cars. The police are standing about, 100s of them. It is a warm evening. The citizens have a meeting using megaphones. There are suggestions, proposals & amendments. Then we move the dirt back onto the roadway with ~~as~~ our hands. Small fistfuls. It is the story of the boy, the bucket & the ocean. It's folksy. It's vital. I am doing it with so many emotions my hands are shaking. Soon the police cars accelerate at us. I trip. I'm nearly run over. Others begin pounding the police cars with lumps of dirt. I hear I am shouting 'Don't'. Some shout with me. Others cheer the pelting of the police cars. I'm suddenly worried about my dog & my bike. The police are deliberately baiting & the demonstrators are falling for it. I stop digging with my fingers. I get my bike and my dog. I am out of the middle of it when a group of cops moves in, pounces on one person and I can see & Vicki beside me can see fists & boots thumping someone in denim. Those closer scream at the injustice of it, the smug brutality. They have an angry, teaseable group of protestors, so powerless they can only play with their hands. All there is is endurance, and it's so hard to endure with an anxiety turning your stomach over. I want to escape but the magnetism of conflict, the importance of being here, the issue itself. The methods of oppression are so snide. I am not alone in that I feel terrified for freaked ~~looks~~ flashes from eye to eye. And it's such a community of strangers, such a social cross-section come together to save the grass, the trees, the air. There's a barbeque, over there some swings & there a kindergarten. At the moment there's moderately bad traffic. Soon there'll be 35,000 new cars a day. The other day it was muggy, people were becoming hysterical & the carbon monoxide count in the air was dangerous, Anne said. Something about the joggers in the park killing themselves. Heading for heart attacks. This is one of the oldest communities in Melbourne, and because of ~~the~~ football club one of the most jingoistic. Collingwood is the sort of place a spontaneous revolution could take place – forgotten untrendy but solid & stubborn. A great mixture of emotions as you stand there lending weight to the side of foresight. The top of the head chattering, I don't want to get arrested,

I don't want to get hurt. But these police do not act as if they care about justice at all. & Anne said, in court the magistrate wasn't either. The coppers all told different stories, patent lies. Pauline gasped in court audibly, lie after lie. It's crazy but one side of politics wants injustice, falseness, madness, repression, great fascistic shows of force. There's a parade of tanks through the city on Saturday starting 10.18 a.m.
It is banal.
It is insidious.
The whole thing is so unheroic.

The Sixth

Another romantic beginning:

The brother & sister sit & burn incense incessantly.

Story finished.

Fraser has baked the dirty bits of the Report on Human relations. Apparently it's political. He's looking for a scapegoat.

But the Commission recommends that between consenting adults sex should be legal i.e. homosexuality & incest. Against prostitution, the hypocrite protests. But we all know about Singapore where he had a public servant dismissed for failing to procure for him.

The Seventh

Stayed in bed all day. Thought about the excitement of expression.
Expression is one thing.
The thing is whether or not Expression is <u>the</u> thing.

"Failure".
Those who have the knowledge are not those who are seen to have it. Authorities are often not fully informed. ARE USUALLY MISINFORMED. Private people are sometimes more informed. Being more loving of their particular taste, they make more time. Bearers of private knowledge are often cynical because they have to to constantly criticise public authority because they happen to know better. They usually double-check their facts. Not necessarily bitterly.
Private knowledge makes it difficult.
Private knowledge somehow makes it worthwhile.
Beyond useful is freedom.
Freedom is not having to but loving to.

Bearing & expanding private knowledge is a reliable enjoyment.
To have the capability of private, reliable enjoyment is a rare & beautiful thing.
Those who suffer from not having private reliable enjoyment because of misbegotten notions of success are not to be felt sorry for.
Those who turn their private enjoyment of knowledge into bitter resentment about not getting success are not to be felt sorry for.
Those who think about deserving will find themselves nose up to the brickwall of unfairness.
Nothing is fair.
To exploit this situation is bad.
This situation is usually exploited under the title of being realistic.
The realist is a shit, & smug complacency is damnation.

The sirens call in the incense burning and the

drapes are camp and calling curtains drapes so camp and they are tastefully anachronistic in fact pretending to live in a period that is not one's own is quaint and camp and not evilly anachronistic.

Anachronism can be bad because it is false & untrue, hence romantic.
Romanticism is not necessarily ordering one's life by the vagaries of the emotions, emotions ought to guage sanity.
To know one is becoming hysterical is so sane.
Hysterics is often a sane response.
Repression of hysterics leads to bigger & worse things.
Bigger & worse things include rape, murder & suicide.
Success finds failure difficult, to understand, to cope with, to be tolerant of.
Failure is a lot of pain.
Choose pain for deeper understanding.
Pain seen from safety vantage is a joy.

Another's pain expressed successfully is not necessarily understood.
Expression is a doing.
A doing is not necessarily a knowledge.
Another's pain used for the success of expression is often done in the arts.
The artist gains.
The sufferer just suffers.
Art as comfort – strange concept.
Such assumptions aren't questioned often enough.
The questioning of assumptions is likely to throw you from the success bracket into the failure bracket.
Such a journey might be the thing.

The thing about handwriting a modern classic is that it is outside the possibility of success.
The question of identity in this case is whether or not one is a writer anyway.
A writer merely puts pen to paper.
Socrates did not.
Wittgenstein did not.

Writers need teachers like Socrates in the market place, in the cafés, in bed and at breakfast.

Writers need to love their teachers.

Writers should not attend universities, but should have free access to libraries & photostat machines.

The be all & end all are somewhere else.

To be involved in realities as such is to be soon bored.

Success must be boring.

To fail in truth is to fall victim to boredom.

To succeed in truth is probably to fail in reality.

To fail in reality is to be constantly on the end of a question.

Things in truth are so bad.

Hysterics are healthy.

Knowledge & pain are superior to smug complacent romance & acceptance of reality.

Romance is lies.

America is good at the romance of lies.

Sentiment is a right wing plot. Just watch T.V.
Crocodile tears set up around invalid pain
situations & happy endings
There are no endings, let alone happy ones.

Life goes on in much the same way & death
can be political.
Socrates' suicide was political.
Plato was a recorder of conversations.
Conversation is the basis of Socratian teaching.

Courage is often a surprise to the courageous.
How to be courageous is a matter of philosophy
Philosophy in action is ultimately political.
Being able to do something is political & falls
left or right according to whether doing it
was your own choice or not.
It appears best to be but to refuse.
To be a humane anarchist probably requires
philosophic courage.
There is a difference between martyrs & victims.

The city sent us mad. We had to go away. We went into the country. We picked a place that seemed remote where a creek & the Thompson branch. A quiet, bushy place with tall bush & clean icy water. We could, i thought, swim, eat fresh fruit & relax. Listen to the birds. Light a camp fire, fry rice etc. Suddenly there was horror, carloads of men, a sprinkling of women. Many different camps of men: guns, trail bikes, cans, cans, stubbies & bottles. Boys sold things to rape the bush with. Come to piss & shoot at anything that moves. What could two lesbians do? From the madness of the Freeway struggle & the police to this. This reality! But Anne is my teacher for this book & we had conversations. That we could not escape is a reflection on our romance. There were two "vanners" there with squeaky clean clothes & a Hi-ace done out a treat, stereo, bar, bed, place for gas barbeque, trail bike, utensils, glasses, chairs. She talking questions like machine gun fire & he bored. Both of them bored, bored but for their superiority over the yobbos & their beers

The car/ the freeway/ the bush/ the petrol/ pollution

The insanity/ the mining companies/ the energy crisis

The profit motive/ the propaganda/ the items/ violence

Sex/ simplicity/ powerlessness/ thou shalt not

Be shot
survive
drink hemlock.

The Eighth

It is not that I have something to say or that the years have rubbed persuasion into my style — too prejudiced & quick to judge to be be totally confident of my logic. I have a kind of spiritual itch. a thing that suggests freedom with more scratching.

I try to plumb my vacuum.

I must eventually write like this – full of flowing doubting, blown ribbons, the shreds of my romantic nature gently structured like a cobweb foundation. If all my attachments were blowing in the wind, if i were severed, I'd be free. Free and full of envy.

Brief tastes of poetry
of manufacture of identity
of strict form :

I received a letter from Jenny M:
"you have too much humour & self-awareness yourself to be trapped in one voice, or one identity (which is not to deny the vital illusion of continuity which maintains the diversity of the self & its imagination & reality)... your poem works as a love poem. I like the fear of beauty on the battlefield ... You do make the person you are speaking to very credible: capricious, reasonable, guarded, intelligent etc. ..."

That kind of response from sister poet could do a person for a lifetime; but the lover herself, how did she respond? 'What's all this shit?' To know where i am i have to attack another, it seems.

From S.M., again: "One of these days I'll dare you to write a totally insincere but not damaging review & publish it. In a few weeks you'll realise that most of it was truer than not. With some urgent & compulsive &/or well-balanced exceptions, sincerity is something that undermines love-affairs & sells American toothpaste. Throw away Jack Falstaff & you throw away the world. (When I said that over-zealous self-realisation was at its best comic I didn't deny that art & humanity at their best can be comic, too."

With this handwritten classic i am thanking you, Jenny — it's a joke. A joke on the M.A. students of the future, they catch me masturbating alone — without relationship, without approval, sans emotionalism. Sans pride, studs & marching boots. Without the probability of M.A.s in the future why bother? But what's approbation, anyway, when you're dead? Success? I write letters because i need answers, my soul needs answers. Letters have done a lot for me. If there were no letters, literature would be truly dead.

Laugh at my popularity. It is Falstaffian and maybe all popularity is — a lying rogue with entertainment value, begging on a grand scale. We're vampires, one & all.

I must go now & sleep with my friend.

The Ninth

Do the old hate the young? A lot of sentiment is involved with thinking & feeling about the aged. They have the power of Reaction, they demand understanding & give none. Power is merely a matter of daring to be obnoxious. Powerlessness is a proclivity towards generosity & selflessness. Now if the Old haven't learnt with all their years the ways of the world & romantically believe in all the false values of sentiment, what happiness can they get? We're not responsible for their unhappiness if we can only give lipservice & charity. If they have chosen to remain ignorant, they abuse their natural power. The cult of Elders, pooh. A wise old person is a rare thing. Most have a lifeload of Fear & Frustration & Guilt, started in youth. I wish it wasn't so when i see the delicate fragility of age.

The cult of the Elders—the cult of the Elders! Now & then you may come across a wise old person but that's very very rare & usually boils down to quaint. The cult of the Elders is a disease so widespread it seems against life itself to question it. All they have is a whole lifeload of Fear, Guilt and frustration, and what little generosity they retain is squashed & squeezed out flat. So, it's Society (who?) which has tipped loads of fear, guilt and frustration on the human ground, and bitterness stands around in mounds like so much uncollected garbage... polluting not only the aged themselves but those over whom they assume power so soon, very soon, youth itself is crabbed with age. 'And there's nothing new under the sun.'

The moral air is filthy.

The moral air is filthy.
The city air is filthy.
The bush is getting it, too.
The only reasonable escape is the effort.
We must confront the corrosion in ourselves.
Suicide beats age, but why should i be logical?
Suicide is an action out of individualism, considering oneself so alienated – a bourgeois individualist decision? Must my despair become total isolation? I've gotta believe in something. Women & their anarchy. Action & intelligence. Inquiry & relationship. Sex & caring. I believe I can give. I can die better than suicide. I know nothing about being tortured in gaol for my beliefs, except Amnesty International's statistics. So my despair is ignorant, also. As my hope is. Life has many livable moments for those with humour.

Judith R. says Finola Moorhead doesn't have

a monopoly on starvation—

(forget the rest of the world, shall we?)—

that when she gained a grant from the Literature Board for $10,000 p.a. she had to give up her academic salary & suffered privation. Fortunately her husband retained his academic salary.

There's got to be a snobbery for the poor. You know something apparently ungraspable by the more privileged. Something big enough in some situations to die for.

But i can't name them.

Here in Australia fascism is insidious, is insidiousness. And brazen & cynical. They can beat you up in the streets. "The police are doing what they can." There's an election tomorrow.

Guess who they'll return.
People are ignorant swine.
They have to be loyal to the liars.
Mungo McCallum counted 69 lies in Fraser's speech at a press conference early December, 1977.

I'll have to care more about past lives than money, no choice really – makes more sense than politics. This thing I'm handwriting for principle's sake has got to be important. The sequence of events in themselves tragic with the objective of moving people & letting them see & feel.

Anne gave me a ring this morning, inscribed 'Fata Morgana' – that's how she sees me. The dog is sick. Thoughts about pain & pleasure. There is no peace & quiet, it's just a mirage. Pleasure is having a shit when you need one. Pain is not.

Then Anne started talking about Virginia Woolf & Simone Weil, their not eating & freaking out about bodily functions. Her theory is that they were repressed dykes. Well, let's take shitting as Eisenstein's "golden section", then their not being able to express their feelings sufficiently, their psyches refusing to & their minds feeding off male philosophy, they are likely to turn against themselves, physically. Like saints, madly. Powerful, brilliant women with a great deal of understanding of a certain sort of pain that is chiefly unfelt as itself, but generalised & broadened becoming inexplicable, too big with knowledge to capture a workable sanity, to let it out, completely. It's all so confusing. Is it better to self-indulge & scream out the pain? One is not the centre of the universe. While there is pain there is choice, but one can't rush around all the time in hysterics, as if our coats were on fire.

we must refuse to.
Such is the political situation.
Relationships are political.
Sex & emotion can light up your coat.
In the inadvertance of going about her
own business, she can set you in flames.

Evolve.
Ignorance is reactionary politics.
Relationships can change your politics.
& pain prevents some ignorance.
If you imagine you have revolutionary
politics & do not feel the pain of them
in your personal life, you are reactionary.
But if you go under in your pain your
politics are ineffective.

The Tenth

Today marks exactly 2 weeks since starting date, and now there's a picture in TIME Dec 5. 1977 of C.S. Lewis 'at ease in his study in the 1940's' in an armchair with books behind him — same as mine at the beginning here, Moorhead '76 by Bernie O'Regan — that makes this a spoof. A scream. Should i bind this up in fireproof material & rush it off to a bank vault, this speedy mistresspiece — hah.

My mother happened to flip through it as we waited for lunch in the city. She pointed out spelling errors. She was repulsed by the subject matter & soon got angry & said it was self-indulgent (she, too, has a horror of bodily functions). She said 'that group of old maids you live with can't even look after a dog'; she had

asked about my dog, who is sick.
She burst into tears of grief about my life, accused me of having no social conscience. Do my new moral values include compassion, consideration & thoughtfulness? She kept sneering at Fata Morgana, the bridal band.

Oh shit. I reject the Institution of the Family. I must.
HAPPINESS IS AN EVENING AT HOME WITH THE FAMILY — on the back window of the car I'm following. Aw Gawd. Couldn't imagine worse. Happiness is deadened emotional commitment. Families all start wrongly with heterosexual monogamy & the children suffer all sorts of resultant tensions arising from that. I'm horrified. I have to rebel against the older generation. Nothing is done to alleviate their ignorance. It all breeds total selfishness & perverted reluctant self-sacrifice

It is so widespread.
Yesterday, the majority of Australian people gave the Fraser fraudulent government a landslide victory. And that's that.

There are lots of short stories about the place. Not to be written unless there's a reason. Money was the noble reason for Checkov's short stories. You read the stories & they are a charm.

All the same self-indulgence beats oppression, compromice & deadened or perverted emotional experience. Incest is not self-indulgence. Incest is a product of the perversity of family life.

The Eleventh

This relationship is like the relationships that didn't happen that happened. This means that the quality of emotion has the quality of imagination. Has that sense of urgency & object. The quality of emotion suggests a discovery. Or further discovery. Importance which vies with other importances. It has to do with character & willed extension of character. A character is something to discover, place for discovery. That's why, in the others that didn't happen, waiting all night on the footpath was unquestionably the right thing to do. The waiting time causes intimacy of thought, hence discovery of the nature of character & its relation to emotion or itself — a kind of worth in living. You don't give in, you articulate the boundaries of your existence, you find the will thus behave. And behaviour expands the very nature of knowledge: emotional investigation.

I'm not talking about self-denial.
For not going into that investigation is not discovering the real mechanics of living. So I reckon. Rationalising those hours. Generosity is often considered waste.

To be outside the general definitions is to be responsible for your own ethics. No judgment.

Thank you Marcuse, I refuse to work — hence forth.
Somehow i ask forgiveness for this refusal. This begging for forgiveness might be the neurotic reason why i turned out "writer" rather than anything else. Public. A something. Before that writing may have been an apology.
But it is true, Anne, I become anxious if i can't write, and the 'can' of that can't is not only time & space but also what

Anxiety about what. Oh gee.

Many of my faults in relating to you are related to my tongue-tied-ness. Need a pen to think & then form & content intrude & lie about the intimate & banal. Vicious neurotic circle. One is two or three steps away from merely being. Simply being. Being in the expressive minute, the immediate, rather than the reflective aftermath.

You don't give me the compliment of 'being real'. Does that make me invalid, unreal, including my emotional make-up, my passion? You say i have no passion?

The Twelth

You know i once loved Eliot — his still point & all that — so he is like a parent whose values i must know in my emotions to reject in my emotions — fully embrace to fully fall away from. That is delicious in art, the pushing away of loving arms, to step higher ... how i bullshit, sire.

This moment of the modern classic is written in a small park bounded by Lygon & Cardigan Streets, Carlton, but i have been reading it & having thoughts of theatre & a select audience.

Popularity is smiles exchanged.
Popularity is trying fairly hard.
Popularity is meeting people in the eye.
Popularity is fairly neurotic.
Popularity is a doubtful quality.
Popularity is a generous face.

Popularity is breaking & entering.
Popularity is drinking & smoking.
Popularity is expecting nothing.
Popularity is having time.
Popularity is being busy.
Popularity is carrying cash.
Popularity is curiosity.
Popularity is insecurity.
Popularity is not knowing exactly what's what.
Popularity is asking answerable questions.
Popularity is concern for people's health.
Popularity is sincere insincerity.
Popularity is hard to achieve inside the system
except among your own kind & then it's how
much you're prepared to give away.

Popularity can be calculated.
People who calculate to be popular might
be unsuccessful in real terms.
Success & popularity are not to be confused.
Popularity is often a matter of opportunity.

(Anne hates my popularity)
A sad melancholy person can be popular.
Repeating a word like popularity become
onomatapoeic. Bubble gum bursts.
Soon one is thinking of weasels.

When i brought up the worth of living question Anne suddenly became loquacious. I accused myself as she spoke of not reaching the same intensity of self-questioning. Maybe i had turned to people. She considered my concept of 'friendship' cheap. She has it in a perspective that i don't. I come on the circus-ring character, I'm opportunistic. You only know through pain & suffering 'It shouldn't have to be that way but this society is so insane it has to be I'm afraid.' P & S friends.

I'm going to tart up these blank pages between cups of coffee & short trips. The rushed thoughts of the lonely effort. The Lonely Effort.

Dear Little Old Lady, in the FAW audience a fortnight ago, with your bags & parcels, your inevitable presence of such gatherings, your dreadful bits of prose, your rhyming poems all rejected by the best most well known publishers, your impolitic raving-on & on about what everyone knows, bless you for thinking i approved of everything you do. Bless your consistent failure. Such failure is not to be felt sorry for.

I told Dorothy that not many people knew the difference between 260 blank pages & 260 written on pages. Critics often don't. She was hurt, she wanted me to see 'flow' in her work, at least in some places. How can you have flow in Bits & Pieces, i asked. I'm sitting there all emotional & caring demolishing her. Anne laughed when i said i did not have the arrogance to do what Dorothy did.
Di says i never <u>do</u> anything.

I write the interruptions &
I write the justifications & I don't dare to write no ordinary diary, how hell i don't like myself enough, aw shit, i've got to call it a modern classic. WORK, a waste of time. a shouted secret ...

confessing hypocrisy doesn't matter. I wanted to learn from the physical fact of doing. I learnt something this morning but i've forgotten what. Why do i think writing is more important than saying? Why did i ask Dorothy her world view? Why do i think philosophy is necessary? She said her book was a tribute to her mother's mind in its time of destruction. I thought the answer inadequate. Why do people sit around tables & talk all day? Why don't people sit at tables & talk more often? When the disputes about language & words are over is there a concurrence on the nature of reality? This is sloppy circling of doubt.

Some of them were stoned & some of them were singing. Casually i washed the dog, took her to the park & came back straight into the conversation. Do i really want to pose the question of Nothing? Question nihilism. Going into seclusion every month, during menstruation, might give a girl time to think.

The wind is making the papers on the wall restless. And that wasn't all.

Anne is always writing in her book, quotes from Wittgenstein, Simone Weil & Herbert Marcuse. I've no one to quote, only Jane Austen & then you might as well read the whole book.

The Thirteenth

i beg your pardon

Imagination is the perception of Reality.

i beg your pardon

If Imagination were but how it would be merely Style.

Definitions of Style are not definitions of Imagination.

Imagination is as is The Memory or The Mind.

"The imagination" is an affectation

Such affectation assists romanticism in its constant fission.

Take away "the", the article, & you have fusion.

Fusion is & is not created.

∴ to use language creatively is to perceive existence.

What is perceived is not a mystery, though it is often unknown.

a mystery is unknowable.

What is unknown, but perceived in some way, is

game for discovery.
The hunt. The hint. The clue. Detection.
The witness of discovery describes good art.
Good art can make of some unknown known.
Pierces reality.
Revelation of reality is like having a deepish obscurity (within oneself) articulated.
Articulation is putting an inner thing outside.
To be placed outside it must have a form which can stand up on its own like a well-balanced sculpture.
The form is in the placing, the presentation, the transubstantiation.
Remaining within, it has no artistic form.
To be put out it must have artistic form.
This placing is creative work.
Which is all not to say you're not creative if you're not placing things all over the place.
Everyone can't make movies: this is a financial truism.
The pressure some of us feel about putting our

inner things out there is largely inexplicable.
Nothing to do with success & lack of it.
That difference gives rise to points of philosophy, social consciousness, personal worth & politics.
Not to mention, money, privilege, capricious fate etc.
Its worth as form is metred by the actual perception of reality.
Reality here is neither realities nor realism.
Perception of reality has to do with personal worth because a yukky person is interested in distorting reality, lying & the propagation of untrue realities.
Anything at all which is put outside & represented which is not the perception of reality aides evil.
This is an unfashionable way of putting it.
Facts are not the whole story.
If one intentionally places bare facts one is likely to misrepresent reality.
One misleads people.

It's not so easy to achieve placement outside, anyway. (there's a lot of rotten writing around & other art work).

Bad (evil & rotten) art has made me angry without my exactly knowing why.

It affected me in the same way as seeing someone kicking dumb animals dogs.

An anger similar to that in response to the inhumane.

Now i see it on the level of propaganda & it's not for the general good

A piss on rotten art.

The realisation of good art is a thrill, it's a help & recharges the creative & imaginative energy: this is generally good.

Okay, FOR THE GENERAL GOOD.

The general good is in each individual.

Knowledge of reality in the individual is good for the mob in that there is an increase in imagination around.

If this knowledge leads to lemming-like mass suicide is it an asset to the general good?

No. My heart says, no.
Such energy be would a force against self destruction, wouldn't it?
Self destruction brings energy down to its carnal element, the whole being the sensually perceived world.
But there is psychic energy & destruction of the physical self would disperse this rather than concentrate & control & enoble it.
We have the mental attributes to do this.
We don't have to fill the ether with more little unhappy ghosts.

Reality is fusion not fission.
Our physical, mental & psychic energies

are intrinsically interlocked.
Suicide ∴ is dispersion not concentration
& mutual self-help.

Has waste anything to do with failure?
If you fail to waste in this society you're
not a success.
Waste requires corruption.
Success is an acceptance of corruption.
Corruption & corruption.
It's a bandwagon.
People are jumping on these bandwagons
all drumming their way to decadence.
When decadence is the rule, the real individual
is likely to fall victim to waste & failure.
When decadence rules, the exceptions sticking
to principles of general good etc. will have
to suffer starvation & other privations.
Unless the exceptions multiply survival is
in jeopardy.
There is the horrific perception of total negation.

This is 1977 & we know about
Black Holes.
We have in our heads this conception of a
solid substance that steals all light &
is nothing.

& decadence is obviously some negation.
Death is not necessarily a negation.

I haven't thought about Death much.

A drunk girl in Lygon St. is staggering
between two companions. She stops outside
the record shop & she yells, hey look
at the spunky arse on this chick, hey
look at the spunky arse on this chick.
Her boyfriends ignore her. And she stays
swaying in front of the window.

Women appreciating women in sexist fashion!!!.

There is a tickle on my tongue
when a moment of love is well brought
up on the screen. It is a different feeling
from being affected by manufactured
sentimentality — slightly, subtly distinct.
Must i question my notions of good
art? Good is such a dangerous, bloody
four-letter word

Is art itself in question?
Anne read me a piece from Simone Weil
about the irresponsibility of the Dadaists, &
something about the Surrealists misrepresenting
reality to no moral purpose.

We might retire into Jane Austen's "business
of the emotions" manipulated to great moral
purpose, but then we must consider her
nobility, class for her, a metaphor for us.
Nobility distinct from snobbery.
Justice for the righteous

well, it's unsafe waters to start
judging art by its perceivable moral purpose.

Mysteries are sacred.

I'm so influenced by her I don't even know what i think anymore. I open my palms & appeal to the audience. (She alone turns her head away in scorn.)

My mother at the Art Gallery looking through Rowse's HOMOSEXUALS IN HISTORY turns to criticise my clothes & hairy armpits in public. It's embarrassing. She said it was the last straw when she saw the look in the Cloakroom man's eyes.

Yesterday a little girl was hit by a car as a direct result of the opening of the Freeway that we, the dreaded extremists, tried to stop. Thank goodness, police have to do point duty.

Met Chris Mann in the Laundromat.
a fitting thing. We exchanged nonbooks.
His is a table cloth, a mat, a wallhanging
with spaces for definition, amendment.
It's a breakfast activity. He estimates it
will take about 2 years to read. Of mine,
the handwritten modern classic, he said,
'a bribe.' Maybe it'll take as long to read
as it does to write.

Laundromat intelligentsia. Roll over de
Beauvoir & Sartre.
Language is the business of the emotions.
Language is the business of politics.
Language is the business of being & not being
with people.
Language is the prospect of the thinker.
Language still has something to do with pen &
paper.
Language not books we're on about.
Mann & Moorhead in the Laundromat agree

that language is imperialist.

I don't dare mention meaning.
Meaning is in the gossipping of hearts.
Meaning is discovering the extent.
Knowing the extent is pretty important.
Beyond the extent is extremism.
Radical eccentricity is essential.
It forwards one not to conform.
Non conformism is not necessarily ego centric.
Ego centrics are old fashioned.

Families & egos are sewn together with
the twine of self-sacrifice & duty.
Self-sacrife has an ego centric base.
Rewards are related to the causal concept.
Causality is a linear view of history.
That is history under laboratory conditions.

Chris flicked something from the edge of the
page & said, Caught one of your fleu de lis.

So ends the handwritten
modern classic, in a laundromat in
Elgin Street.

And Anne, if you ever read this,
know that my love for you enabled
me to learn so much, & be so brave – not
brave enough for you, but brave
for me –

17th December 1977

Finola Moorhead.